KINGFISHER
Larousse Kingfisher Chambers Inc.
95 Madison Avenue
New York, New York 10016

First American edition 1995
2 4 6 8 10 9 7 5 3 1
This selection copyright © Larousse plc 1995
Illustrations copyright © Susan Field 1995

LIBRARY OF CONGRESS CATALOGING-IN-PUBLICATION DATA
The little book of love / compiled by Caroline Walsh: illustrated by
Susan Field.—1st American ed.
1. Love poetry.   2. Children's poetry.   3. Nursery rhymes.
[1. Love—Poetry.   2. Poetry—Collections.]   I. Walsh, Caroline,
II. Field, Susan, ill.
PN6110.L6L45   1995
808.81'9354—dc20   94-26328   CIP   AC

ISBN 1 85697 535 5

Printed in Hong Kong

# THE LITTLE BOOK OF

# LOVE

*Selected by Caroline Walsh • Illustrated by Susan Field*

Kingfisher

NEW YORK

# Contents

$T$rue love is but a humble
    low-born thing,
And hath its food served up in
    earthen ware;
It is a thing to walk with,
    hand in hand,
Through the every-dayness of
    this work-day world.

JAMES RUSSELL LOWELL
from 'True Love'

If you think that you're in love,
But still there is some question,
Don't worry much about it,
It may be indigestion.

ANON

If you love me, love me true, Send me a ribbon and let it be blue.

CHOCOLATE
CHOCOLATE
                    i

love
              you so
                    i

want
        to

marry
        you
        and

live
        forever
                    in the
                    flavor

of your
brown

ARNOLD ADOFF

Do you carrot all for me?
My heart beets for you,
With your turnip nose
And your radish face.
You are a peach.
If we cantaloupe,
Lettuce marry;
Weed make a swell pear.

ANON

### Sew a Coat for my Love

Sew a coat for my love
take the sun for cloth
cut the moon for lining
put the clouds for padding
borrow the sea-spray for thread
use the stars for buttons
and make the buttonholes of me

ARMENIAN FOLK SONG

## SONNET FROM THE PORTUGUESE

How do I love thee? Let me count the ways.
I love thee to the depth and breadth and height
My soul can reach, when feeling out of sight
For the ends of Being and ideal Grace.
I love thee to the level of everyday's
Most quiet need, by sun and candlelight.
I love thee freely, as men strive for Right;
I love thee purely, as they turn from Praise.
I love thee with the passion put to use
In my old griefs, and with my childhood's faith.
I love thee with a love I seemed to lose
With my lost saints,—I love thee with the breath,
Smiles, tears, of all my life!—and, if God choose,
I shall but love thee better after death.

ELIZABETH BARRETT BROWNING

I'll love you dear, I'll love you
    Till China and Africa meet
And the river jumps over
    the mountain
And the salmon sings in
    the street.

I'll love you till the ocean
    Is folded and hung up to dry
And the seven stars go squawking
    Like geese about in the sky.

W.H. AUDEN
from 'As I Walked Out One Evening'

Roses are red,
Violets are blue,
Sugar is sweet,
And so are you.

Do you love me
or do you not?
You told me once
But I forgot.

22

Just as the vine
Grows round the stump,
You are my darling
    Sugar lump.

Just as the mouse
Runs over the rafter,
You are the very one
I'm after.

23

### I WILL GIVE MY LOVE AN APPLE

I will give my love an apple without e'er a core,
I will give my love a house without e'er a door,
I will give my love a palace wherein she may be,
And she may unlock it without any key.

My head is the apple without e'er a core,
My mind is the house without e'er a door,
My heart is the palace wherein she may be,
And she may unlock it without any key.

ANON

Shall I compare thee to a summer's day?
Thou art more lovely and more temperate:
Rough winds do shake the darling buds of May,
And summer's lease hath all too short a date:
Sometime too hot the eye of heaven shines,
And often is his gold complexion dimm'd:
And every fair from fair sometime declines,
By chance, or nature's changing course, untrimm'd.
But thy eternal summer shall not fade
Nor lose possession of that fair thou owest;
Nor shall death brag thou wanderest in his shade,
When in eternal lines to time thou growest;
So long as men can breathe, or eyes can see,
So long lives this, and this gives life to thee.

WILLIAM SHAKESPEARE

## A DITTY

My true-love hath my heart, and I have his,
By just exchange one to the other given:
I hold his dear, and mine he cannot miss,
There never was a better bargain driven:
　　My true-love hath my heart, and I have his.

His heart in me keeps him and me in one,
My heart in him his thoughts and senses guides:
He loves my heart, for once it was his own,
I cherish his because in me it bides:
　　My true-love hath my heart, and I have his.

SIR PHILIP SIDNEY

LOVE WITHOUT HOPE

Love without hope, as when the young bird-catcher
Swept off his tall hat to the Squire's own daughter,
So let the imprisoned larks escape and fly
Singing about her head, as she rode by.

ROBERT GRAVES

## Folk Song from Fukushima

Handsome boy!
O for a thread
To haul him over
To my side!

ANON
17th century, translated from the Japanese.

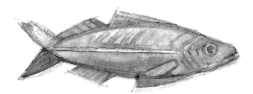

IMPOSSIBILITIES TO HIS FRIEND

My faithful friend, if you can see
The Fruit to grow up, or the Tree:
If you can see the color come
Into the blushing Pear, or Plum;
If you can see the water grow
To cakes of Ice, or flakes of Snow:
If you can see, that drop of rain
Lost in the wild sea, once again:
If you can see, how Dreams do creep
Into the Brain by easy sleep:
Then there is hope that you may see
Her love me once, who now hates me.

ROBERT HERRICK

It's once I courted as pretty a lass,
    As ever your eyes did see;
But now she's come to such a pass,
    She never will do for me.
She invited me to her own house,
    Where oft I'd been before,
And she tumbled me into the hog-tub,
    And I'll never go there any more.

TRADITIONAL

1.

2.

3.

4.

## RIDDLE-ME-REE

My first is in life (not contained within heart)
My second's in whole but never in part.
My third's in forever, but also in vain.
My last's in ending, why not in pain?

LIZ LOCHHEAD

Is love the answer?

You say you have been drenched
        waiting for me
on the foothill-trailing mountain.
O that I could be
that trickling rain!

PRINCE OTSU
3rd century Chinese poet

I know you little, I love you lots,
My love for you would fill ten pots,
Fifteen buckets, sixteen cans,
Three teacups, and four dishpans.

ANON

One I love, two I love,
   Three I love, I say,
Four I love with all my heart,
   Five I cast away;
Six he loves, seven she loves, eight both love.
   Nine he comes, ten he tarries,
Eleven he courts, twelve he marries.

TRADITIONAL

43

## Absence and the Wind

Blow, northern wind,
Send thou me my sweeting,
Blow, northern wind,
Blow, blow, blow.

ANON

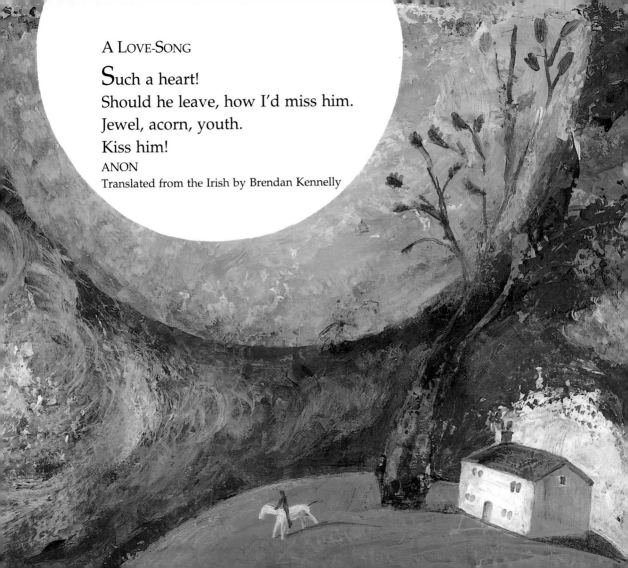

A Love-Song

Such a heart!
Should he leave, how I'd miss him.
Jewel, acorn, youth.
Kiss him!

ANON
Translated from the Irish by Brendan Kennelly

### She Who Is Always In My Thoughts

She who is always in my thoughts prefers
Another man, and does not think of me.
Yet he seeks for another's love, not hers;
And some poor girl is grieving for my sake.
    Why then, the devil take
Both her and him; and love; and her; and me.

BHARTRHARI
(7th century translated from the Sanskrit)

## CURLY LOCKS

Curly locks, Curly locks,
    Wilt thou be mine?
Thou shalt not wash dishes
    Nor yet feed the swine,
But sit on a cushion
    And sew a fine seam,
And feed upon strawberries,
    Sugar and cream.

TRADITIONAL

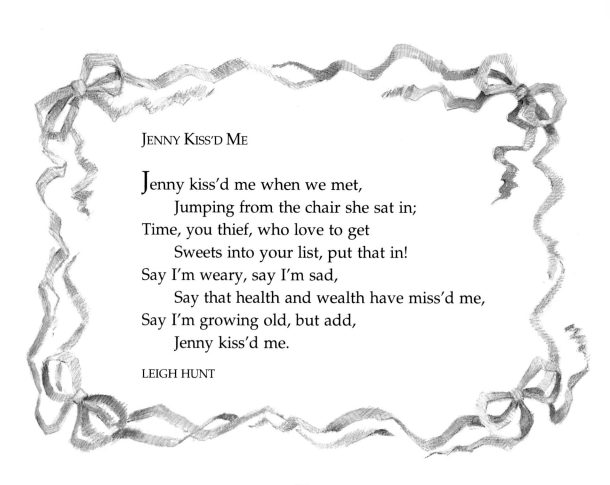

### Jenny Kiss'd Me

Jenny kiss'd me when we met,
    Jumping from the chair she sat in;
Time, you thief, who love to get
    Sweets into your list, put that in!
Say I'm weary, say I'm sad,
    Say that health and wealth have miss'd me,
Say I'm growing old, but add,
    Jenny kiss'd me.

LEIGH HUNT

## WELL CAUGHT

These days I'm in love with my face.
It has grown round and genial as I've become older.
In it I see my grandfather's face and that
Of my mother. Yes—like a ball it has been thrown
From one generation to the next.

GERDA MAYER

## CATS

Those who love cats which do not even purr,
Or which are thin and tired and very old,
Bend down to them in the street and stroke their fur
And rub their ears and smooth their breast, and hold
Their paws, and gaze into their eyes of gold.

FRANCIS SCARFE

## ODE TO AN EXTINCT DINOSAUR

Iguanodon, I loved you,
With all your spiky scales,
Your massive jaws,
Impressive claws
And teeth like horseshoe nails.

Iguanodon, I loved you.
It moved me close to tears
When first I read
That you've been dead
For ninety million years.

DOUG MacLEOD

# IGUANODON

Iguanodon

[Cretaceous

beak.

Iguanodon tooth

10

long

spike

thumb.

hind legs

tail

big toes,

EXTINCT DINOSAUR

LOVE ME—I LOVE YOU

Love me—I love you,
    Love me, my baby;
Sing it high, sing it low,
    Sing it as may be.

Mother's arms under you;
    Her eyes above you;
Sing it high, sing it low,
    Love me—I love you.

CHRISTINA ROSSETTI

## Index of Authors and First Lines

## Acknowledgments

For permission to reproduce copyright material, acknowledgment and thanks are due to the following:

Arnold Adoff for "Chocolate Chocolate" from *Eats* by Arnold Adoff, copyright © 1979 by Arnold Adoff; 10 lines from "As I Walked Out One Evening" from *The English Auden: Poems, Essays & Dramatic Writings* 1927-1923 by W. H. Auden, edited by Edward Mendelson, copyright © by Edward Mendelson, William Meredith, and Monroe E. Spears, executors of the Estate of W. H. Auden, reprinted by permission of Random House Inc.; Penguin Books Ltd. for "She who is always in my thoughts" by Bharthari from *Poems from the Sanskrit* translated by John Brough (Penguin Classics, 1968) copyright © John Brough 1968; Brendan Kennelly for "A Love-Song" translated from the Irish by Brendan Kennelly from *The Penguin Book of Irish Verse* edited by Brendan Kennelly, published by Penguin Books Ltd.; Polygon for "Riddle-Me-Ree" from *Dreaming of Frankenstein* by Liz Lochhead; Penguin Books Australia Ltd. for "Ode to an Extinct Dinosaur" from *In the Garden of Bad Things* by Doug MacLeod; Blackie Children's Books for "Well Caught" by Gerda Mayer from *You Just Can't Win* selected by Brian Moses, published in 1991; Reed Consumer Books Ltd. for "Cats" from *Underworlds* by Francis Scarfe, published by William Heinemann Ltd; HarperCollins Inc for "Huckleberry, Gooseberry, Raspberry Pie" from *Father Fox's Penny Rhymes* by Clyde Watson, copyright © Clyde Watson 1971.

Every effort has been made to obtain permission from copyright holders. If, regrettably, any omissions have been made, we shall be pleased to make suitable corrections in any reprint.